The
Scuppernong Press
Wake Forest, NC

Living in the Land of Cotton Biography Series

Abraham Lincoln:
A Man of Contradictions

By
Richard Lee Montgomery

Living in the Land of Cotton Biography Series
Abraham Lincoln: A Man of Contradictions

©2018 Richard Lee Montgomery

First Printing

The Scuppernong Press
PO Box 1724
Wake Forest, NC 27588
www.scuppernongpress.com

Cover and book design by Frank B. Powell, III

All rights reserved. Printed in the United States of America.

No part of this book may be reproduced or transmitted in any form or by any means, electronic or mechanical, including photocopying, recording, or by any information and storage and retrieval system, without written permission from the editor and/or publisher.

International Standard Book Number ISBN 978-1-942806-14-1

Library of Congress Control Number: 2018931148

Living in the Land of Cotton Biography Series

— Table of Contents —

Introduction to Series .... *iii*

Introduction 1

Lincoln's Formative Years 5

Lincoln's Religious Affections 10

Lincoln and the People of Color 21

Concluding Thoughts 29

Bibliography 33

— Introduction to Series —

As a member of the Sons of Confederate Veterans and for every other member, we have been charged to stand in *"the defense of the Confederate soldier's good name, the guardianship of his history, the emulation of his virtues, the perpetuation of those principles which he loved."* Through my website, the books I have published and the lectures I have given, are all about keeping the Confederate culture alive in this cynical time of America's history.[1]

For my life, I have committed it to living a lifestyle which would be pleasing to the Lord Jesus Christ. However, knowing that I can easily displease Him and therefore diminish His glory, there are foundational tools which have been a constant reminder for me in seeking to glorify my God. Seeking to live for the Lord Jesus Christ, I have learned to strive in developing a prayer life and equally allowing a healthy time in the reading of the Word of God, which can bring direction and focus.

My point is, this can easily describe many of the leaders of the Confederacy as well as those on the battlefield as soldiers. In fact, the Confederate Constitution teaches to us what was of most importance to them, *"We, the people of the Confederate States, each State acting in its sovereign and independent character, in order to form a permanent federal government, establish justice, insure domestic tranquility and secure the blessings of liberty to ourselves and our posterity — invoking the favor and guidance of Almighty God — do ordain and establish this Constitution for the Confederate States of America."*[2]

---

[1] livinginthelandofcotton.com
[2] Constitution of the Confederate States of America (Milledgeville: Georgia State Convention, 1861), 2.

I find the phrase *"invoking the favor and guidance of Almighty God,"* as a foundational statement in this new constitution. It teaches us there was a culture which was very important to the South before, during and after the years of 1861-1865. In this new series of biographies, the reader will see that there were men and women who fought for the protection of their families, homes, towns, cities, states and country by an invading army. The reader will see there were those who held to Christian principles and at the same time, fought for States' Rights and held this principle high.

I am not suggesting that this new government was a Christian (theocratic) nation because there were many who were not Christians, but who also fought for States' Rights. Also, there were many who did not know anything about this constitutional right issue — they just knew they did not want anyone dictating to them and their families what they can and cannot do.

This series is based on primary sources. By that I mean they are books published before "Lincoln's War" and books published going into the 1930s. Much of what you will read are quotes and narratives from these sources. At times, I will interject my thoughts but centered on what the source stated. The desired outcome for this new series is that the reader might be inspired, encouraged and become more proactive for the truths of history.

I hope you enjoy this biography,

Richard Lee Montgomery

Living in the Land of Cotton Biography Series

Abraham Lincoln

Born: February 12, 1809, Hardin County, Kentucky.

Wife: Mary Todd Lincoln.

Children: Robert Todd, William Wallace, Tad, Edward Baker.

Death: April 14, 1865, Ford's Theater, Washington, DC.

Buried: Oak Ridge Cemetery, Springfield, Illinois.

— Introduction —

When studying any branch of history, whether it be world, national, state or local, the student can easily find discrepancies in the composition, based on conflicting accounts or the interpretation of the writer.

Living in the Land of Cotton Biography Series

One of the best examples in this dilemma is found in the areas of biographies. Thus, we come to the man — Abraham Lincoln.

One account tells us he was an honest man. Many writings teach us he was a Christian man. I mean, look at the plethora of times he quoted the Scripture. A great deal of narratives has given us a very persuasive writing of Lincoln's love for the Negro population, which obviously, they say, was the motivation to freeing the slaves.

In Memory of Abraham Lincoln. *The Reward of the Just*, 1865

There is an old term which needs to come to the forefront and it is the word apotheosis. In the 1845 Webster's Dictionary, we are given this definition: [AP-O-THEO-SIS] *"Deification; consecration; the act of placing a prince, or other distinguished person, among the heathen deities."* [3] Then, in the 1884 Webster's Dictionary it says, *"Act of elevating a mortal to the rank of the gods."* [4] This definition is easily applied to what we have been taught for the last one hundred and fifty years plus concerning the man Abraham Lincoln.

Meriwether

Elizabeth Avery Meriwether tells us, *"After Lincoln's death, and the apotheosis ceremony had been performed, it became the custom of Republican writers and speakers to talk of 'Lincoln's being in touch with the people.' This is nothing but apotheosis twaddle. Lincoln was no more in touch with the common people than he was with the distinguished*

---

[3] Noah Webster, *An American Dictionary of the English Language* (New York: Harper & Brothers, 1845), 44.
[4] Dorsey Gardner, *Webster's Practical Dictionary* (New York: Ivison, Blakeman, Taylor & Company, 1884), 19.

leaders of his own party. It is almost the unanimous testimony of Republicans who knew the living Lincoln that he was neither trusted or beloved by the people of any class. Stanton, when on his death-bed, told General Piatt that the common soldiers in the army had to be warned by their officers not to manifest their dislike to Lincoln when he came to review them." [5]

Another term which needs to be defined is "contradiction." The 1845 Webster's Dictionary tells us: "*1. An assertion of the contrary to what has been said or affirmed; denial; contrary declaration. 2. Opposition, whether by words, reproaches or attempts to defeat. 3. Direct opposition or repugnancy; inconsistency with itself; incongruity or contrariety of things, words, thoughts or propositions.*" [6]

John Russell Young [7] makes an intriguing statement concerning Abraham Lincoln.: *"I have never read a description of him that recalls him as I knew him. Something always beyond and beyond. Nor has fame been kind to him in the sense that fame is never kind unless it is just. There is little justice in much that is written of Lincoln. Then comes the dismal fear that he is to live in an apotheosis.'*

Young

And the reviewer goes on, *'If Lincoln could have chosen, Mr. Young thinks, and justly, that he would have desired to be remembered as he was, and not looked at through any distorting medium like the aureole and crowning flame of martyrdom. … Mr. Lincoln did not impress the capital as a welcome personal force. Living in an element*

---

[4]Elizabeth Avery Meriwether (Pseudonym, George Edmonds), *Facts and Falsehoods Concerning the War on the South, 1861-1865* (Memphis: A. R. Taylor & Company, 1904), 163.
[6]Noah Webster, *An American Dictionary of the English Language* (New York: Harper & Brothers, 1845), 187.
[7]Journalist, author, diplomat, and the seventh Librarian of the United States Congress.

of detraction, he was not a popular man. It would be hard to recall his friends." [8]

Allen Thorndike Rice[9] describes the process of apotheosis this way: *"Story after story, and trait after trait, as varying in value as in authenticity, have been added to the Lincolniana until at last the name of the great War President has come to be a biographical lodestone, attracting without … discrimination both the true and the false."* [10] That is what we have been fed from our history books for more than one hundred and fifty years. That is why there is a need to take a second, third, fourth, etc., look at the man — Abraham Lincoln. Some say the narrative in which we have been taught for all these years, makes it a daunting exercise or maybe an impossible endeavor to expose this tool called apotheosis, the making of Abraham Lincoln something that he was not.

Well, it can be done and the best tool to do this, is by using primary sources. What did the books of that day say of these men and women, both in the North and the South? What did these men and women say of their lives through their books and writings? Primary sources is the position we need to find ourselves, when seeking to find the truth, with the aim to defend the Confederate soldier's good name and work towards *"the guardianship of his history, the emulation of his virtues, the perpetuation of those principles which he loved."* [11]

---

[8] Charles Landon Carter Minor, *The Real Lincoln: From the Testimony of His Contemporaries* (Richmond: Everett Waddey Company, 1904), 206.
[9] Journalist and the Editor and Publisher of the *North American Review* from 1876 to 1889.
[10] Charles Landon Carter Minor, *The Real Lincoln: From the Testimony of His Contemporaries* (Richmond: Everett Waddey Company, 1904), 202.
[11] S. A. Cunningham, Editor and Proprietor, Index: *Confederate Veteran*, Published Monthly in the Interest of Confederate Veterans and Kindred Topics, Volume XIV (Nashville, 1906), 255.

Also, when taking on this task, you will find that Abraham Lincoln did not try to hide the events of his life or the things he said and believed, even when it contradicts our history books. For all these long years of the monotonous teaching and the retelling of the same story of exaltation of a man, who, according to many of the writers and witnesses of his day, say otherwise. There must be a paradigm shift in the teaching of "Lincoln's War."

— Lincoln's Formative Years —

> "Mr. Davis told Dr. Egerton that in a private and confidential talk which he had with Mr. Lincoln the latter told him that he was of Southern extraction; that his right name was, or ought to have been Enloe, but he had always gone by the name of his step-father.
>
> Mr. Enloe's Christian name was Abram, and if Mr. Lincoln was his son he was not unlikely named for him." [12]

The first contradiction in Abraham Lincoln's life is found at the beginning of his life — his birth. Traditionally we have been taught Abraham Lincoln's father and mother were Thomas and Nancy Hanks Lincoln and his sister was Sarah. Maybe so — maybe no. Perhaps a second look is needed?

Let's start with **James Caswell Coggins** who documented this narrative: "*Some time in the early fifties two young men of Rutherford County, NC, moved to Illinois and settled in or near Springfield. One of them,*

---

[12] James Caswell Coggins, *Abraham Lincoln: A North Carolinian With Proof* (Gastonia: Carolina Printing Company, 1927), 129.

Coggins

whose name was Davis, became intimately acquainted with Mr. Lincoln. In the fall of 1860, just before the presidential election, Mr. Davis and his friend paid a visit back to Rutherford and spent a night with Dr. Egerton. Of course the candidates for the presidency would be discussed. Mr. Davis told Dr. Egerton that in a private and confidential talk which he had with Mr. Lincoln the latter told him that he was of Southern extraction; that his right name was, or ought to have been Enloe, but that he had always gone by the name of his step-father.

Mr. Enloe's Christian name was Abram, and if Mr. Lincoln was his son he was not unlikely named for him."[13]

Cathey

North Carolinian **James Harrison Cathey** tells this in his book entitled, *The Genesis of Lincoln: Truth is Stranger Than Fiction*: "Mr. Ragland is a citizen of Missouri and a leading attorney of the town of Stockton. He wrote: 'In reply to your letter to my wife have to say: About twelve years ago I called on Col. T. G. C. Davis at his office in St. Louis, Mo. At that time I lived in Illinois. Col. Davis was a relative of mine, his mother having been a Miss Ragland of Kentucky. Col. Davis was also born in Kentucky, and was a cousin of Jeff Davis, President of the Confederacy.

Col. Davis having once resided for a long while in Illinois, the conversation naturally turned upon her times and men. He said he was personally and intimately acquainted with President Lincoln — was often associated with him, as well as against him, in law cases before the Supreme Court of Illinois; that they, as members of a committee of the Constitutional

---

[13] Ibid., 129.

Living in the Land of Cotton Biography Series

Convention (I think of 1844 or 5) of Illinois, drafted the most of the Constitution. He said that he knew the mother of Lincoln; that he was raised in the same neighborhood in Kentucky, and that it was generally understood, without question, in that neighborhood, that Lincoln, the man that married the President's mother, was not the father of the President) but that his father's name was Enloe. These facts I have a distinct recollection of. Col. Davis died about three years ago, in Denton, Texas.'" [14]

Another historical narrative which continues to be held from the history books once again given to us by **James Caswell Coggins**. *"Mr. Collins is fifty-six years of age and resides in the town of Clyde, in Haywood County, NC. He served three years of the War Between the States as a private, after which he was promoted to the second lieutenancy of his company, in which capacity he continued until the surrender. He has been in the mercantile business for twenty-five years, ten years of which he was a traveling salesman. He is now proprietor of a hardware store in his home town. He is well known over the entire western part of the State as a gentleman of the most unquestionable integrity.*

Coggins

He said: 'The first I knew of any tradition being connected with Abraham Lincoln's origin on his father's side was in 1867. At that time I was in Texas, and while there I made the acquaintance of Judge Gilmore, an old gentleman who lived three miles from Fort Worth.

He told me he knew Nancy Hanks before she married, and that she then had a child she called 'Abraham.' Judge Gilmore said she married a man by the name of Lincoln, a whisky distiller. Lincoln he said, was a very poor man, and they lived in a small log house.

---

[14] James H. Cathey, *The Genesis of Lincoln: Truth is Stranger Than Fiction* (Atlanta: Franklin Printing and Publishing Company, 1899), 77-78.

After Nancy Hanks was married to Lincoln, said Gilmore, the boy was known by the name of Abraham Lincoln. He said that Abraham's mother, when the boy was about eight years old, died. Judge Gilmore said he himself was five or six years older than Abraham Lincoln; that he knew him well; attended the same school with him. He said Lincoln was a bright boy and learned very rapidly; was the best boy to work he had ever known.

He said he knew Lincoln until he was almost grown, when he, Gilmore, moved to Texas. During his residence in Texas he was elected judge of the county court. He was an intelligent, responsible man. Years ago I was traveling for a house in Knoxville. On Turkey Creek, in Buncombe County, North Carolina, I met an old gentleman whose name was Phillis Wells. He told me that he knew Abraham Lincoln was the son of Abraham Enloe, who lived on Ocona Lufta.

Wells said he was then ninety years of age. When he was a young man he traveled over the country and sold tinware and bought furs, feathers and ginseng for William Johnston, of Waynesville, NC. He said he often stopped with Abraham Enloe. On one occasion he called to stay over night, as was his custom, when Abraham Enloe came out and went with him to the barn to put up his horse, and while there Enloe said: My wife is mad; about to tear up the place; she has not spoken to me in two weeks, and I wanted to tell you about it before you went into the house. Then, remarked Wells: I said what is the matter? And Abraham Enloe replied: The trouble is about Nancy Hanks, a hired girl we have living with us Wells said he stayed all night, and that Mrs. Enloe did not speak to her husband while he was there. He said he knew Nancy Hanks there, that she was a good looking girl, and seemed to be smart for business.

Wells said before he got back there on his next trip that Abraham Enloe had sent Nancy Hanks to Jonathan's Creek and hired a family there to take care of her; that later a child was born to Nancy Hanks, and she named him Abraham. Meantime the trouble in Abraham Enloe's family *had not abated. As soon as Nancy Hanks was able to travel, Abraham Enloe hired a man to take her and her child out of the country, in order to restore quiet and peace at home. He said he sent her to some of his relatives near the state line in Kentucky. He said Nancy and the child were cared for by Enloe's relatives until she married a fellow by the name of Lincoln.*

I asked the old gentleman if he really believed Abraham Lincoln was the son of Abraham Enloe, and he replied: I know it, and if I did not know it I would not tell it. I made special inquiry about the character of Wells, and everyone said that he was an honest and truthful man and a good citizen." [15]

These sources are only given as evidence to show or to teach, that indeed Abraham Lincoln was a man of contradiction. It is true much which has been taught in public and private schools, as well as in the institutes of higher learning, would refrain from identifying these sources and quotes as a part of history. For that — contradictions in the life of Lincoln have and will continue to plague us without the fuller story of his formative years.

---

[15]James Caswell Coggins, *Abraham Lincoln: A North Carolinian With Proof* (Gastonia: Carolina Printing Company, 1927), 132-135.

Living in the Land of Cotton Biography Series

— Lincoln's Religious Affections —

"God knows I would be one. Yes, God knows I would be one were I convinced that Christianity is true, but not convinced of its truth, I am an unbeliever." [16]

Mary Lincoln

Another contradiction in the Lincoln *apotheosis* is found in what we have been taught about his religion. All these years we have heard, "Abraham Lincoln was a fine and faithful Christian man" or "Lincoln loved and quoted the Bible often." Well, as a foundation for exposing way of thinking, we quickly run into conflicting statements from Lincoln's wife, **Mary Todd Lincoln**. She says, "Mr. Lincoln once remarked to a friend that his religion was like that of an old man named Glenn, in Indiana, whom he heard speak at a church meeting, and who said: 'When I do good, I feel good; when I do bad, I feel bad; and that's my religion.' Mrs. Lincoln herself has said that Mr. Lincoln had no faith — no faith, in the usual acceptance of those words. 'He never joined a church; but still, as I believe, he was a religious man by nature. He first seemed to think about the subject when our boy Willie died, and then more than ever about the time he went to Gettysburg; but it was a kind of poetry in his nature, and he never was a technical Christian.'" [17]

---

[16] John E. Remsburg, *Abraham Lincoln: Was He A Christian* (New York: The Truth Seeker Company, 1893), 46.
[17] Alexander K. McClure, *Abe Lincoln's Yarns and Stories: A Complete Collection of the Funny and Witty Anecdotes That Made Lincoln Famous as America's Greatest Story Teller* (Henry Neil, 1901), 386.

So, what is a "technical Christian?" The word "Christian" is used three times in the New Testament:

> Acts 11:26 – *"and when he had found him, he brought him to Antioch. And for an entire year they met with the church and taught considerable numbers; and the disciples were first called Christians in Antioch."* [18]

> Acts 26:28 – *"Agrippa replied to Paul, "In a short time you will persuade me to become a Christian."* [19]

> 1 Peter 4:16 – *"but if anyone suffers as a Christian, he is not to be ashamed, but is to glorify God in this name."* [20]

A good working definition of the term "Christian" comes from the "William Smith's Dictionary of the Bible, Volume 1," published in 1889. It states: *"The disciples, we are told (Acts xi. 26), were first called Christians at Antioch on the Orontes, somewhere about A.D. 43. The name, and the place where it was conferred, are both significant. It is clear, that the appellation 'Christian' was one which, though eagerly adopted and gloried in by the early followers of Christ, could not have been imposed by themselves. They were known to each other as brethren of one family, as disciples of the same Master, as believers in the same faith, and as distinguished by the same endeavors after holiness and consecration of life; and so were called brethren (Acts XV. 1, 23; 1 Cor. vii. 12), disciples (Acts ix. 26, xi. 23), believers (Acts v. 14), saints (Rom. viii. 27, XV. 25)."* [21]

The Bible is very clear in its teaching in the description of a born again Christian and how they must examine themselves according to Scripture. In 1 John 5:13, believers are told, *"These things I have written to*

---

[18] The Holy Bible: Updated New American Standard Bible (Grand Rapids: Zondervan Publishing House, 1999), 941.
[19] Ibid., 957.
[20] Ibid., 1036.
[21] H. B. Hackett, *Dr. William Smith's Dictionary of the Bible, Volume 1* (A to Gennesaret, Land of) (Boston: Houghton, Mifflin & Company, 1889), 428.

you who believe in the name of the Son of God, so that you may know that you have eternal life." [22] As a guide, every born again believer is to live with the desire to please the Lord Jesus Christ, which then loudly confirms their affections for Him and Him alone. In other words, the Christian life is to live out Christ in their lives, with the hope of glorifying Him. Now remember, the task before us, is to investigate Lincoln's religious affections and conclude, whether those affection were demonstrated or lived out, in Christ. To be a Christian is not because you call yourself one or because of the good deeds you do or the church you go to. It is a way of life, living for Jesus Christ and Him alone.

A good question for every born again Christian to ask, as we must do on the life of Lincoln is, "did Lincoln enjoy having fellowship with Christ and His redeemed people?" Scripture teaches us in 1 John 1:3, *"What we have seen and [ourselves] heard, we are also telling you, so that you too may realize and enjoy fellowship as partners and partakers with us. And [this] fellowship that we have [which is a distinguishing mark of Christians] is with the Father and with His Son Jesus Christ (the Messiah)."* [23]

Also, from the Bible, we are told that for man to have fellowship with the *"Father and His Son Jesus Christ,"* a person must receive the mercy and grace of God, which only comes through Jesus Christ and only Him. Acts 4:12 tells us, *"And there is salvation in no one else; for there is no other name under heaven that has been given among men by which we must be saved."* [24]

Now — now we come to the task in matching these Biblical tenants to the life of Lincoln in his religious affections concerning Christ and how he talked of Him. Once again, **Ward Hill Lamon**, who was Lincoln's

---

[22] The Holy Bible: Updated New American Standard Bible (Grand Rapids: Zondervan Publishing House, 1999), 1041.
[23] The Amplified Bible Large Print (Grand Rapids: Zondervan Publishing House, 1987), 1893.
[24] The Holy Bible: Updated New American Standard Bible (Grand Rapids: Zondervan Publishing House, 1999), 931.

self-appointed bodyguard and later biographer, made this astute observation of his boss. He said, *"Mr. Lincoln was never a member of any church, nor did he believe in the divinity of Christ, or the inspiration of the Scriptures in the sense understood by evangelical Christians. His theological opinions were substantially those expounded by Theodore Parker. Overwhelming testimony out of many mouths, and none stronger than that out of his own, place these facts beyond controversy.*

Lamon

When a boy, he showed no sign of that piety which his many biographers ascribe to his manhood. His stepmother — herself a Christian, and longing for the least sign of faith in him — could remember no circumstance that supported her hope. On the contrary, she recollected very well that he never went off into a corner, as has been said, to ponder the sacred writings, and to wet the page with his tears of penitence. He was fond of music; but Dennis Hanks is clear to the point that it was songs of a very questionable character that cheered his lonely pilgrimage through the woods of Indiana. When he went to church at all, he went to mock, and came away to mimic. Indeed, it is more than probable that the sort of 'religion' which prevailed among the associates of his boyhood impressed him with a very poor opinion of the value of the article. On the whole, he thought, perhaps, a person had better be without it." [25]

Hanks

Growing into his adulthood and with Lincoln's ambitions for politics, we are given this narrative by **Josiah Gilbert Holland** who was briefly the editor-in-chief of the *Springfield Republican* and gives this account of a discussion he and Lincoln had: *"****Newton Bateman****, Superintendent of Public Instruction for the State of Illinois, occupied a room adjoining*

---

[25] Ward H. Lamon, *The Life of Abraham Lincoln: From His Birth To His Inauguration As President* (Boston: James R. Osgood & Company, 1872), 486-487.

Holland

and opening into the Executive Chamber. Frequently this door was open during Mr. Lincoln's receptions; and throughout the seven months or more of his occupation Mr. Bateman saw him nearly every day. ... **Often when Mr. Lincoln was tired he closed his door against all intrusion, and called Mr. Bateman into his room for a quiet talk.** ... Toward the close of October, and only a few days before the election. Calling Mr. Bateman to a seat at his side, having previously locked all the doors, he said: 'let us look over this book. I wish particularly to see how the ministers of Springfield are going to vote.' In that manner they went through the book, and then he closed it and sat silently and for some minutes regarding a memorandum in pencil which lay before him. At length he turned to Mr. Bateman with a face full of sadness, and said: 'Here are twenty-three ministers, of different denominations, and all of them are against me but three; and here are a great many prominent members of the churches, a very large majority of whom are against me. Mr. Bateman, I am not a Christian God knows I would be one but I have carefully read the Bible, and I do not so understand this book. ... [26] Just making the statement "I am not a Christian" should be enough to convinced us that Abraham Lincoln did not have an affection for Christ.

Bateman

Also, from Lincoln's third and last law partner and biographer, **William Henry Herndon,** tells us, "*Lincoln was very politic, and a very shrewd man in some particulars. When he was talking to a Christian, he adapted himself to the Christian. When he spoke to, or joked to one of his own kind, he was indecently vulgar. Hence the different opinions*

---

[26] J. G. Holland, *The Life of Abraham Lincoln* (Springfield, Mass.: Gurdon Bill, 1866) 236-237.

about Mr. Lincoln's Christianity and vulgarity. Mr. Lincoln was chaste in his ideas and language when it was necessary, and when not so he was vulgar in his jokes and stories; he was at moments, as it were, a Christian, through politeness, courtesy, or good breeding toward the delicate, tender, nerved man, the Christian, and in two minutes after, in the absence of such men, and among his own kind, the same old unbeliever. I have witnessed this it may be a thousand times. This conduct of Mr. Lincoln was not hypocritical, but sprang from a high and tender regard for the feelings of men." [27]

Herndon

Herndon consistently stays with his personal convictions on Lincoln's religion by giving this account, "As to Mr. Lincoln's religious views, he was, in short, an infidel, ... a theist. He did not believe that Jesus was God, nor the Son of God, — was a fatalist, denied the freedom of the will. Mr. Lincoln told me a thousand times, that he did not believe the Bible was the revelation of God, as the Christian world contends. The points that Mr. Lincoln tried to demonstrate (in his book)[28] were: First, That the Bible was not God's revelation; and. Second, That Jesus was not the Son of God. I assert this on my own knowledge, and on my veracity. **Judge Logan, John T. Stuart, James H. Matheny**, and others, will tell you the truth. I say they will confirm what I say, with this exception, — they all make it blacker than I remember it. **Joshua F. Speed** of Louisville, I think, will tell you the same thing." [29]

Logan, Stuart & Matheny

---

[27] William Henry Herndon, *The Religion of Abraham Lincoln* (Plainfield, N. J., 1915), 66-67.
[28] A small pamphlet Lincoln wrote with his thoughts on Christianity and was thrown quickly in the fire after his employer Samuel Hill read it.
[29] Ward H. Lamon, *The Life of Abraham Lincoln: From His Birth To His Inauguration As President* (Boston: James R. Osgood & Company, 1872), 489.

Living in the Land of Cotton Biography Series

Speed

William Henry Herndon confirms this account: "*In 1834, while still living in New Salem and before he became a lawyer, he was surrounded by a class of people exceedingly liberal in matters of religion. Volney's '***Ruins***' and Paine's '***Age of Reason***' passed from hand to hand, and furnished food for the evening s discussion in the tavern and village store. Lincoln read both these books and thus assimilated them into his own being. He prepared an extended essay called by many, a book in which he made an argument against Christianity, striving to prove that the Bible was not inspired, and therefore not God's revelation, and that Jesus Christ was not the son of God. The manuscript containing these audacious and comprehensive propositions he intended to have published*

Hill

or given a wide circulation in some other way. He carried it to the store, where it was read and freely discussed. His friend and employer, **Samuel Hill**, *was among the listeners, and, seriously questioning the propriety of a promising young man like Lincoln fathering such unpopular notions, he snatched the manuscript from his hands and thrust it into the stove. The book went up in flames, and Lincoln's political future was secure. But his infidelity and his sceptical views were not diminished. He soon removed to Springfield, where he attracted considerable notice by his rank doctrine. Much of what he then said may properly be credited to the impetuosity and exuberance of youth. One of his closest friends, whose name is withheld, narrating scenes and reviewing discussions that in 1838 took place in the office of the county clerk, says: 'Sometimes Lincoln bordered on atheism. He went far that way, and shocked me. I was then a young man, and believed what my good mother told me . ... He would come into the clerk's office where I and some young men were writing and staying, and would bring the Bible with him; would read a chapter and argue against it. ... Lincoln was enthusiastic in his infidelity. As he grew older he grew more discreet; didn't talk much before strangers about his religion; but to friends, close and bosom ones, he was* *always open and avowed, fair and honest; to strangers, he held them off from policy.'* **John T. Stuart**, who was Lincoln's first partner, substantially endorses the above. *'He was an avowed and open infidel, declares Stuart,' and sometimes bordered on atheism; ... went further against Christian beliefs and doctrines and principles than any man I ever heard; he shocked me. I don t remember the exact line of his argument; suppose it was against the inherent defects, so-called, of the Bible, and on grounds of reason. Lincoln always denied that Jesus was the Christ of God denied that Jesus was the son of God as understood and maintained by the Christian Church.'* **David Davis**[30] tells us this: *'The idea that Lincoln talked to a stranger about his religion or religious views, or made such speeches and remarks about it as are published, is to me absurd. I knew the man so well; he was the most reticent, secretive man I ever saw or expect to see. He had no faith, in the Christian sense of the term had faith in laws, principles, causes and effects.'* Another man[31] testifies as follows: *'Mr. Lincoln told me that he was a kind of immortalist; that he never could bring himself to believe in eternal punishment; that man lived but a little while here; and that if eternal punishment were man's doom, he should spend that little life in vigilant and ceaseless preparation by never-ending prayer.'* Another intimate friend furnishes this: *'In my intercourse with Mr. Lincoln I learned that he believed in a Creator of all things, who had neither beginning nor end, possessing all power and wisdom, established a principle in obedience to which worlds move and are upheld, and animal and vegetable life come into existence. A reason he gave for his belief was that in view of the order and harmony of all nature which we behold, it would have been more miraculous to have come about by chance than to have been created and arranged by*

Stuart

Davis

---

[30]David Davis was a United States Senator from Illinois and associate justice of the United States Supreme Court.
[31]William H. Hannah.

Fell

some great thinking power. As to the Christian theory that Christ is God or equal to the Creator, he said that it had better be taken for granted; for by the test of reason we might become infidels on that subject, for evidence of Christ's divinity came to us in a somewhat doubtful shape; but that the system of Christianity was an ingenious one at least, and perhaps was calculated to do good.' **Jesse W. Fell**, *to whom Lincoln first confided the details of his biography, furnishes a more elaborate account of the latter's religious views than anyone else. In a statement made September 22, 1870, Fell says: 'If there were any traits of character that stood out in bold relief in the person of Mr. Lincoln they were those of truth and candor. He was utterly incapable of insincerity or professing views on this or any other subject he did not entertain. Knowing such to be his true character, that insincerity, much more duplicity, were traits wholly foreign to his nature, many of his old friends were not a little surprised at finding in some of the biographies of this great man statements concerning his religious opinions so utterly at variance with his known sentiments. True, he may have changed or modified these sentiments*[32] *after his removal from among us, though this is hardly reconcilable with the history of the man, and his entire devotion to public matters during his four years residence at the national capital. It is possible, however, that this may be the proper solution of this conflict of opinions; or it may be that, with no intention on the part of any one to mislead the public mind, those who have represented him as believing in the popular theological views of the times may have misapprehended him, as experience shows to be quite common where no special effort has been made to attain critical*

---

[32]"EXECUTIVE MANSION, WASHINGTON, May 27, 1865.
'FRIEND HERNDON: Mr. Lincoln did not to my knowledge in any way change his religious ideas, opinions, or beliefs from the time he left Springfield to the day of his death. I do not know just what they were, never having heard him explain them in detail; but I am very sure he gave no outward indication of his mind having undergone any change in that regard while here.'
Yours truly,
JOHN G. NICOLAY."

accuracy on a subject of this nature. This is the more probable from the well-known fact, that Mr. Lincoln seldom communicated to any one his views on this subject; but be this as it may, I have no hesitation whatever in saying that whilst he held many opinions in common with the great mass of Christian believers, he did not believe in what are regarded as the orthodox or evangelical views of Christianity." [33]

Another gentleman, **Daniel Webster Wilder**, served as the secretary of the Osawatomie Convention, that organized the Republican Party in Kansas and traveled through the state with Abraham Lincoln. Wilder was the editor of the *Leavenworth Conservative,* an anti-slavery paper, and wrote and published an editorial on Lincoln's religious views, in which he affirmed Lincoln was a disbeliever in Christianity. In his editorial Wilder said, *"Lincoln believed in God, but not in the divinity of Christ. At first, like Franklin, he was probably an Atheist. Although a forgiving man himself, he did not believe that any amount of penitence could affect the logical effects of violated law."* [34]

Wilder

To be a Christian is not confirmed by making the statement, "I am a Christian." It is not based on the exercise of going to church or telling others that you come from a "Christian family." To be "in Christ" or to be a redeemed and regenerated sinner is to have a changed life spiritually, evidenced by a life of living faith. **John Gill** explains it this way, *"yet the life of faith does not consist in works, but in special acts of it on its proper object, Christ; and a temporary faith is only an assent to the truth*

Gill

---

[33] William H. Herndon and Jesse William Wiek, *Herndon's Lincoln: The True Story of a Great Life, Volume 3* (Springfield: The Herndon's Lincoln Publishing Company, 1889), 439-443.
[34] John B. Bramsburg, *Abraham Lincoln: Was He A Christian?* (New York: The Truth Seeker Company, 1893), 214.

of some propositions concerning Christ; but is not as saving faith, a going out unto him, depending on him and believing in him, for the salvation of the soul." [35] Point is, the Christian life is a dependent life on Christ, seeking to glorify Him and Him alone. Mr. Wilder's statement, *"Lincoln believed in God, but not in the divinity of Christ,"* [36] describes a religion that does not seek to glorify God through Christ.

---

[35] John Gill, *The Cause of God and Truth. In Four Parts* (London: Bradbury & Evans, Printers, 1838), 250.
[36] John B. Bramsburg, *Abraham Lincoln: Was He A Christian?* (New York: The Truth Seeker Company, 1893), 214.

Living in the Land of Cotton Biography Series

— Lincoln and People of Color —

"I will say, then, that I am not, nor ever have been, in favor of bringing about in any way the social and political equality of the white and black races; that I am not, nor ever have been, in favor of making voters or jurors of negroes, nor of qualifying them to hold office, or intermarry with the white people; and I will say in addition to this that there is a physical difference between the white and black races which I believe will forever forbid the two races living together on terms of social and political equality." [37]

For many, Abraham Lincoln has been taught in our education system, that he was the Great Emancipator. According the 1845 Webster's, we are given this definition of *Emancipation*: "One who emancipates or liberates from bondage or restraint." [38] Maybe a broader understanding is needed.

"*Emancipate:* To release from slavery, oppression, or other evil; to liberate or set free." [39]

"EMANCIPATION: An act by which a person who was once in the power of another is rendered free." [40]

---

[37] Arthur Brooks Lapsley, *The Writings of Abraham Lincoln, Volume 5* (G.P. Putnam's Sons, 1906), 35.
[38] Noah Webster, *An American Dictionary of the English Language* (New York: Harper & Brothers, 1845), 291.
[39] Harold Wheeler, *The Waverley Pictorial Dictionary, Volume 3* (DRY-HARK) (London: The Waverley Book Company, 1877), 1376.
[40] John Bouvier, *A Law Dictionary, Adapted to the Constitution and Laws of the United States, Volume 1* (Philadelphia: J. B. Lippincott & Company, 1880), 522.

Living in the Land of Cotton Biography Series

Emancipation is what Abraham Lincoln is remembered for and credited with — freeing the slaves in America. In his "Emancipation Proclamation Speech," Lincoln tells us that he freed all the slaves living within the borders of the Confederate States, which was a completely separate country and government, and he had no jurisdictions over. Point is — those he could not free, he deemed free and for those he could have freed in the North, he said nothing about. And yes, there were slaves in the North. **Mildred Lewis Rutherford** reminds us with this statement, *"They do not tell that General Grant, a slaveholder, was put as leader of the Northern Army and General Lee, who had freed his slaves, as the leader of the Southern Army, but they do say that the war was fought to hold the slaves yet do not tell that only 200,000 slaveholders were in the Southern Army, while 315,000 slaveholders were in the Northern Army."* [41]

Rutherford

Miller

To further support Mrs. Rutherford's remarks, we need to hear **Hugh Gordon Miller**, a lawyer from Norfolk, Virginia, who served as Special Assistant to the Attorney General of the United States. Before the Senate on Friday, May 9, 1952, he ends a speech saying, *"Now, in closing, I have only time to make two points clear, but those two points are vital and elementary to this subject. First, the War Between the States was not fought primarily over slavery. Even Gen. Ulysses S. Grant, during the war, is recorded as having said. 'If I thought that I was fighting to free the slaves, I would sheathe my sword and go home.' Abraham Lincoln, before the war began, in his speech at Peoria, IL, and before he became involved in the expediencies incident to his campaign for*

---

[41]Mildred Lewis Rutherford, *Truths of History: A Fair, Unbiased, Impartial, Unprejudiced and Conscientious Study of History. Object: To Secure a Peaceful Settlement of the Many Perplexing Questions Now Causing Contention Between the North and the South* (Athens, Georgia, 1920), iv.

president, declared, 'If I were a Southerner, I would do just what they are doing,' referring to the slavery issue. Actually, there were 315,000 Negro slave owners fighting in the northern Army, compared to only 200,000 in the Confederate Army.

The Proclamation of Emancipation was war a measure penned in the midst of the war, and aimed not at the whole country equally, but at the seceding States." [42]

It really is elementary — Lincoln did not have some great affection for the Negro people. In fact, primary sources teach us otherwise. For him, it was only a political move to sway the Northern people to coerce the Southern States back into the Union. His concern for the people of color can only be fictitious. Let's examine the primary sources to better understand Lincoln's view of race, directed toward the Negro people.

Lincoln

Abraham Lincoln gave a speech on September 16, 1859, in the city of Columbus, Ohio. It first needs to be said that Mr. Lincoln never tried to hide his true feelings on the race issue. When he broaches the subject in 1859, he is very clear and concise when discussing the equality of the black man and the white man. In the third paragraph of this speech he says, *"I will say here, while upon this subject, that I have no purpose directly or indirectly to interfere with the institution of slavery in the States where it exists. I believe I have no lawful right to do so, and I have no inclination to do so. I have no purpose to introduce political and social equality between the white and the black races. There is a physical difference between the two which, in my judgment, will probably forbid their ever living together upon the footing of perfect equality. ..."* [43]

---

[42] United States of America Congressional Record: *Proceedings and Debates of the 82d Congress, Second Session, Volume 98, Part 9* (March 6, 1952 to April 28, 1952), A2850.

[43] Arthur Brooks Lapsley, *The Writings of Abraham Lincoln, Volume 5* (G.P. Putnam's Sons, 1906), 34.

Later in the speech he says, "*While I was at the hotel to-day an elderly gentleman called upon me to know whether I was really in favor of producing perfect equality between the negroes and white people. While I had not proposed to myself on this occasion to say much on that subject, yet, as the question was asked me, I thought I would occupy perhaps five minutes in saying something in regard to it. I will say, then, that I am not, nor ever have been, in favor of bringing about in any way the social and political equality of the white and black races; that I am not, nor ever have been, in favor of making voters or jurors of negroes, nor of qualifying them to hold office, or intermarry with the white people; and I will say in addition to this that there is a physical difference between the white and black races which I believe will forever forbid the two races living together on terms of social and political equality. And inasmuch as they can not so live, while they do remain together there must be the position of superior and inferior, and I, as much as any other man, am in favor of having the superior position assigned to the white race.*" [44]

After all these years, having been taught that Lincoln was a friend to the black and slave population, we must rethink this schooling. According to *Webster's Dictionary*, the term *teach* means, "*To instruct; to inform; to communicate to another the knowledge of that of which he was before ignorant.*" [45] With that said, we must conclude that much of the Lincolnology that we have been taught, along with the faulty claims of his life. Maybe the question that needs to be asked is: Does this not perpetuate double ignorance, "*where a man is ignorant of his ignorance?*" [46]

Plato's thoughts on "double ignorance" states it this way: "*Ignorance, however, may be conveniently divided by the legislator into two sorts: There is simple ignorance, which is the source of lighter offenses, and double ignorance which is accompanied by conceit of wisdom; and he who is under the influence of the latter, fancies that he knows all about matters*

---

[44]Ibid., 35.
[45]Noah Webster, *An American Dictionary of the English Language* (New York: Harper & Brothers, 1845), 827.
[46]Wolfgang Mieder, *A Dictionary of American Proverbs* (Oxford University Press, 1992), 540.

of which he knows nothing." ⁴⁷ It is like a teacher dispensing faulty information or inaccurate knowledge to a student and continues to spread it to others from there. It's like not being aware of one's ignorance while thinking that one knows. This is what has happened for more than one hundred and fifty years — a perpetuation of ignorance.

Perhaps **William Cowper** says it best — poetically, *"Thou may'st of double ignorance boast. Who know'st not that thou nothing know'st."* ⁴⁸
Well, anyway, just know, that having created this apotheosis, this deification of a man, calling him the greatest president, honest Abe, the great liberator or emancipator has done a great disservice to the history of our country. There is a desperate need for a turnaround in the teaching on the life of "Abraham Lincoln."

Cowper

There is one more thing that needs to be addressed, concerning Lincoln. And it is this — his involvement and endorsement of "colonization." **John Thomas Richards**, former president of the Chicago Bar Association of 1903 and author of *Abraham Lincoln: The Lawyer-Statesman* tells us, *"The utterances of Mr. Lincoln, both before and after his election to the presidency, indicate clearly that he was a believer in the colonization of the colored people. He sincerely believed that their happiness and the peace of the Republic could be best secured by the separation of the white and the colored races."* ⁴⁹

Richards

---

⁴⁷C. H. A. Bulkley, *Plato's Best Thoughts* (New York: Charles Scribner's Sons, 1883), 235.
⁴⁸H. Stebbing, *The Complete Poetical Works of William Cowper, Volume 1* (New York: D. Appleton & Company, 1852), 268.
⁴⁹John T. Richards, *Abraham Lincoln: The Lawyer-Statesman* (Boston: Houghton Mifflin Company, 1916), 115.

Mr. Richards also tells us, "*On August 14, 1862, addressing a deputation of colored men, President Lincoln expressed clearly his belief that the colonization of that race would be the wisest solution of the difficulties which he foresaw would grow out of the emancipation of the race. In the course of that address he said: — We have between us a broader difference than exists between almost any other two races. Whether it is right or wrong I need not discuss, but this physical difference is a great disadvantage to us both, as I think. Your race suffer very greatly, many of them, by living among us, while ours suffer from your presence. In a word, we suffer on each side. If this is admitted, it affords a reason, at least, why we should be separated. ... It is better for us, therefore, to be separated.*" [50]

It was not just during the "War of Northern Aggression" that Lincoln spoke out on this topic but he was very consistent in what he said before the war. In a speech on June 26, 1857 in Springfield, Illinois Lincoln said, "*... the two races living together on terms of social and political equality.*" In that address said with strong conviction, "*I have said that the separation of the races is the only perfect preventive of amalgamation. I have no right to say all the members of the Republican party are in favor of this, nor to say that as a party they are in favor of it. There is nothing in their platform directly on the subject. ... Such separation, if ever effected at all, must be effected by colonization; and no political party, as such, is now doing anything directly for colonization. Party operations at present only favor or retard colonization incidentally. The enterprise is a difficult one; but 'where there is a will there is a way,' and what colonization needs most is a hearty will. Will springs from the two elements of moral sense and self-interest. Let us be brought to believe it is morally right, and at the same time favorable to, or at least not against, our interest to transfer the African to his native clime, and we shall find a way to do it, however great the task may be.*" [51]

---

[50] Ibid., 116.
[51] Arthur Brooks Lapsley, *The Writings of Abraham Lincoln*, Volume 5 (G.P. Putnam's Sons, 1906), 306.

Living in the Land of Cotton Biography Series

Even Lincoln's two biographers, **John George Nicolay** and **John Milton Hay** clearly describes his political creed, *"The political creed of Abraham Lincoln embraced among other tenets, a belief in the value and promise of colonization as one means of solving the great race problem involved in the existence of slavery in the United States. ... Without being an enthusiast, Lincoln was a firm believer in colonization."* [52]

John George Nicolay (Left)
John Milton Hay (Right)

One more fact, that many may not be aware of — Abraham Lincoln, the "Great Emancipator," was a regional manager for the Illinois State Colonization Society. There were eleven managers for this society in the state and on January 26, 1857, Lincoln was elected as one of those leaders. It was recorded in the *Illinois State Journal* and then published in the *Illinois State Journal*, January 28, 1857: *"According to notice, the Illinois State Colonization Society held its annual meeting on Monday evening the 26th, in the Hall of the House of Representatives. In the absence of the president, (Governor Matteson,) Rev. Dr. McMastors, of Alton, took the chair. Prayer was offered, after which the minutes of the last annual meeting and last meeting of the Board of managers were read. Managers, Rev. J. H. Brown, D. D., Rev. S. W. Ilarkey, D. D., Rev. J. W. Pierson, Rev. C. W. Sears, Rev. N. W. Miner, Rev. A. Hale, Wm. Yates Esq., J. S. Vredenburg, Esq., Jas. Thayer, Esq., Hon. S. M. Collum, Hon. A. Lincoln."* [53]

Carl Sandburg was an American poet, writer, and editor who won three Pulitzer Prizes: two for his poetry and one for his biography of Abraham Lincoln. Sandburg was considered as an expert on Abra-

---

[52] Beverley Bland Munford, *Virginia's Attitude Toward Slavery and Secession* (New York: Longmans, Green & Company, 1909), 77-78.
[53] *Illinois State Journal, Volume 9*, Number 186, 28 January 1857, page 4.

Sandburg

ham Lincoln. In fact, Sandburg gave a speech on Abraham Lincoln in a Joint Session of Congress of the United States in 1959. The introduction for Sandburg was given by the Speaker of the House **Sam Rayburn** of Texas who stated, *"And now it becomes my great pleasure, and I deem it a high privilege, to be able to present to you the man who in all probability knows more about the life, the times, the hopes; and the aspirations of Abraham Lincoln than any other human being. He has studied and has put on paper his conceptions of the towering figure of this great and this good man. I take pleasure and I deem it an honor to be able to present to you this great writer, this great historian, Carl Sandburg."* [54]

Rayburn

As an expert on Abraham Lincoln's life, Sandburg makes a very pointed comment — he says, *"Of new and old societies, unions, lodges, churches, it seemed that Lincoln belonged only to the Whig party and the American Colonization Society."* [55]

---

[54] Carl Sandburg, *Abraham Lincoln: The Prairie Years And The War Years* (New York: Dell Publishing Company, 1960), 10.
[55] Carl Sandburg, *Abraham Lincoln: The Prairie Years And The War Years* (New York: Dell Publishing Company, 1960), 195-196.

Living in the Land of Cotton Biography Series

— Concluding Thoughts —

"Lincoln was a man of many moods. He reacted differently to different stimuli, and to the same stimulus at different times. His feelings ran the gamut from abysmal dejection to rollicking gaiety: and he never revealed his whole nature to any one man nor showed the whole of his nature at any one time. He cannot be judged by the mechanical tests of a rigid consistency: for he was not that kind of man.

… Such a nature and character seem full of contradictions; and a man who is subject to such transitions will always be a mystery to those who do not know him wholly. Thus no two men among his intimate friends will agree concerning him." [56]

So here we are — Abraham Lincoln, a man of contradictions. For so long he has been pictured and described as an example for all of mankind. You pick the age group: childhood, teen or adult and he fits the bill.

The above quote comes from **Dr. Josiah Gilbert Holland** but we need to read more of what he said: *"The writer has conversed with multitudes of men who claimed to know Mr. Lincoln intimately; yet there are not two of the whole number who agree in their estimate of him. The fact was that he rarely showed more than one aspect of himself to one man. He opened himself to men in different directions. It was rare that he exhibited what was religious in him; and he never did this at all, except*

Holland

---

[56] William E. Barton, *The Soul of Abraham Lincoln* (New York: George E. Doran Company, 1920), 102.

when he found just the nature and character that were sympathetic with that aspect and element of his character. A great deal of his best, deepest, largest life he kept almost constantly from view, because he would not expose it to the eyes and apprehension of the careless multitude.

To illustrate the effect of the peculiarity of Mr. Lincoln's intercourse with men, it may be said that men who knew him through all his professional and political life have offered opinions as diametrically opposite as these, viz: that he was a very ambitious man, and that he was without a particle of ambition; that he was one of the saddest men that ever lived, and that he was one of the jolliest men that ever lived; that he was very religious, but that he was not a Christian; that he was a Christian, but did not know it; that he was so far from being a religious man or a Christian that 'the less said upon that subject the better' that he was the most cunning man in America, and that he had not a particle of cunning in him; that he had the strongest personal attachments, and that he had no personal attachments at all only a general good feeling toward everybody; that he was a man of indomitable will, and that he was a man almost without a will; that he was a tyrant, and that he was the softest-hearted, most brotherly man that ever lived; that he was remarkable for his pure-mindedness, and that he was the foulest in his jests and stories of any man in the country; that he was a witty man, and that he was only a retailer of the wit of others; that his apparent candor and fairness were only apparent, and that they were as real as his head and his hands; that he was a boor, and that he was in all essential respects a gentleman; that he was a leader of the people, and that he was always led by the people; that he was cool and impassive, and that he was susceptible of the strongest passions. It is only by tracing these separate streams of impression back to their fountain that we are able to arrive at anything like a competent comprehension of the man, or to learn why he came to be held in such various estimation. Men caught only separate aspects of his character only the fragments that were called into exhibition by their own qualities." [57]

---

[57] J. G. Holland, *Life of Abraham Lincoln* (Springfield, Mass.: Gurdon Bill, 1866), 241-242.

So, who was Abraham Lincoln? Well, we know he was the president of the United States and that he would do anything to keep the Union together, even if it meant coercion of his citizens, as he called them. Lincoln believed it was a Civil War and not a conflict between two separate countries. Now, important here is an understanding or a working definition of the phrase "civil war." It is *"a war between citizens of the same country."* [58] Noah Webster defines it as *"war between two factions of the same country."* [59] Plain and simple, that's why Yankee's have always called it a Civil War in text books and movies all these years.

Webster

But — it was not a civil war. It was not a war between citizens of the same country. The Confederate States of America was a national government and had a constitution, congress, and capitol. Bottom line — Abraham Lincoln was indeed a man of contradiction, which means we have been taught, in many way, false narrative of his life. Will there be a correction of these things? — likely not — but for those who choose to fight this uphill battle without seeking to give a fuller story, be reminded it is a worthy cause to speak out for a truthful history.

In closing, Henry Johnson, who was a Professor of History at Columbia University, Teachers College gives us this illustrative definition of "History" by saying, *"The original of the word 'history,' a creation of the Greeks, had, however, from the beginning a more serious meaning. It is applied in Homer to the examination of evidence in a legal dispute. A case is brought before a man of skill who 'inquires into the alleged facts and decides what the true facts are.' Historie, in early Greek usage, meant such an inquiry, or any inquiry designed to elicit truth, hence the knowledge so obtained, information on any subject."* [60]

---

[58] Robert Hunter & Charles Morris, *Universal Dictionary of the English Language, Volume 1* (New York: Peter Fenelon Collier, Publisher, 1898), 1030.
[59] Noah Webster, *Webster's New Illustrated Dictionary* (New York: Syndicate Publishing Company, 1911), 227.
[60] Henry Johnson, *Teaching of History in Elementary and Secondary Schools* (New York: The MacMillan Company, 1915), 19.

Living in the Land of Cotton Biography Series

— Bibliography —

Constitution of the Confederate States of America (Milledgeville: Georgia State Convention, 1861).

Illinois State Journal, Volume 9, Number 186, 28 January 1857.

The Amplified Bible Large Print (Grand Rapids: Zondervan Publishing House, 1987).

The Holy Bible: Updated New American Standard Bible (Grand Rapids: Zondervan Publishing House, 1999).

United States of America Congressional Record: Proceedings and Debates of the 82d Congress, Second Session, Volume 98, Part 9 (March 6, 1952 to April 28, 1952).

Barton, William E., *The Soul of Abraham Lincoln* (New York: George E. Doran Company, 1920).

Bouvier, John, *A Law Dictionary, Adapted to the Constitution and Laws of the United States, Volume 1* (Philadelphia: J. B. Lippincott & Company, 1880).

Bulkley, C. H. A., *Plato's Best Thoughts* (New York: Charles Scribner's Sons, 1883).

Bramsburg, John B., *Abraham Lincoln: Was He A Christian?* (New York: The Truth Seeker Company, 1893).

Cathey, James H., *The Genesis of Lincoln: Truth is Stranger Than Fiction* (Atlanta: Franklin Printing and Publishing Company, 1899).

Living in the Land of Cotton Biography Series

Coggins, James Caswell, *Abraham Lincoln: A North Carolinian With Proof* (Gastonia: Carolina Printing Company, 1927).

Cunningham, S. A., Editor and Proprietor, Index: *Confederate Veteran, Published Monthly in the Interest of Confederate Veterans and Kindred Topics*, Volume XIV (Nashville, 1906).

Gardner, Dorsey, *Webster's Practical Dictionary* (New York: Ivison, Blakeman, Taylor & Company, 1884).

Gill, John, *The Cause of God and Truth. In Four Parts* (London: Bradbury & Evans, Printers, 1838).

Hackett, H. B., *Dr. William Smith's Dictionary of the Bible, Volume 1 (A to Gennesaret, Land of)* (Boston: Houghton, Mifflin & Company, 1889).

Herndon, William Henry, *The Religion Of Abraham Lincoln* (Plainfield, N. J., 1915).

Herndon, William H. and Jesse William Wiek, *Herndon's Lincoln: The True Story of a Great Life, Volume 3* (Springfield: The Herndon's Lincoln Publishing Company, 1889).

Holland, J. G., *The Life of Abraham Lincoln* (Springfield, Mass.: Gurdon Bill, 1866).

Hunter, Robert & Charles Morris, *Universal Dictionary of the English Language, Volume 1* (New York: Peter Fenelon Collier, Publisher, 1898).

Johnson, Henry, *Teaching of History in Elementary and Secondary Schools* (New York: The MacMillan Company, 1915).

Lapsley, Arthur Brooks, *The Writings of Abraham Lincoln, Volume 5* (G.P. Putnam's Sons, 1906).

Living in the Land of Cotton Biography Series

Lamon, Ward H., *The life of Abraham Lincoln: From His Birth To His Inauguration as President* (Boston: James R. Osgood & Company, 1872).

McClure, Alexander K., *Abe Lincoln's Yarns and Stories: A Complete Collection of the Funny and Witty Anecdotes That Made Lincoln Famous as America's Greatest Story Teller* (Henry Neil, 1901).

Meriwether, Elizabeth Avery (Pseudonym, George Edmonds), *Facts and Falsehoods Concerning the War on the South, 1861-1865* (Memphis: A. R. Taylor & Company, 1904).

Mieder, Wolfgang, *A Dictionary of American Proverbs* (Oxford University Press, 1992), 540.

Minor, Charles Landon Carter, *The Real Lincoln: From the Testimony of His Contemporaries* (Richmond: Everett Waddey Company, 1904).

Munford, Beverley Bland, *Virginia's Attitude Toward Slavery and Secession* (New York: Longmans, Green & Company, 1909).

Remsburg, John E., *Abraham Lincoln: Was He A Christian* (New York: The Truth Seeker Company, 1893).

Richards, John T., *Abraham Lincoln: The Lawyer-Statesman* (Boston: Houghton Mifflin Company, 1916).

Rutherford, Mildred Lewis, *Truths of History: A Fair, Unbiased, Impartial, Unprejudiced and Conscientious Study of History. Object: To Secure a Peaceful Settlement of the Many Perplexing Questions Now Causing Contention Between the North and the South* (Athens, Georgia, 1920).

Sandburg, Carl, *Abraham Lincoln: The Prairie Years And The War Years* (New York: Dell Publishing Company, 1960).

Living in the Land of Cotton Biography Series

Stebbing, H., *The Complete Poetical Works of William Cowper, Volume 1* (New York: D. Appleton & Company, 1852).

Webster, Noah, *An American Dictionary of the English Language* (New York: Harper & Brothers, 1845).

Wheeler, Harold, *The Waverley Pictorial Dictionary, Volume 3* (DRY-HARK) (London: The Waverley Book Company, 1877).

Living in the Land of Cotton Biography Series

www.ingramcontent.com/pod-product-compliance
Lightning Source LLC
Chambersburg PA
CBHW071548080526
44588CB00011B/1829